Discard

The United States

Wyoming

Paul Joseph
ABDO & Daughters

visit us at
www.abdopub.com

Published by Abdo & Daughters, 4940 Viking Drive, Suite 622, Edina, Minnesota 55435.
Copyright © 1998 by Abdo Consulting Group, Inc., Pentagon Tower, P.O. Box 36036,
Minneapolis, Minnesota 55435 USA. International copyrights reserved in all countries.
No part of this book may be reproduced in any form without written permission from the
publisher.

Printed in the United States.

Cover and Interior Photo credits: Peter Arnold, Inc., SuperStock, Archive, Corbis-
Bettmann

Edited by Lori Kinstad Pupeza
Contributing editor Brooke Henderson
Special thanks to our Checkerboard Kids—Aisha Baker, Morgan Roberts, Tyler Wagner

All statistics taken from the 2000 census; The Rand McNally Discovery Atlas of The
United States.

Library of Congress Cataloging-in-Publication Data

Joseph, Paul, 1970-
    Wyoming / Paul Joseph.
    p. cm. -- (The United States)
    Includes index.
    Summary: Surveys the people, geography, and history of Wyoming, one of the
    biggest states in land size but the smallest in population.
    ISBN 1-56239-802-4
    1. Wyoming--Juvenile literature. [1. Wyoming.] I. Title. II. Series: United
    States (Series)
    F761.3.J67 1998
    978.7--dc21   97-40234
                                                            CIP
                                                           AC

Contents

Welcome to Wyoming

The wonderful state of Wyoming sits midway between the Mississippi River and the Pacific Ocean. In Wyoming, the Great Plains of the West come together with the towering Rocky Mountains. Because of that, the state has an average elevation of 6,700 feet (2,040 m)—higher than every other state but Colorado.

Wyoming is known for its beautiful and different kinds of land. The snow covered mountains, the deserts, canyons, rich farm land, valuable **minerals**, and clear lakes and rivers fill up Wyoming's big land.

In land size, Wyoming is one of the biggest states in the country. However, in **population**, Wyoming is the very smallest. The state doesn't even have 500,000 people living in it. Most large cities in the United States have more than 500,000 people.

Because of its beauty, history, and many things to do, Wyoming attracts many visitors. People visit the state to see the scenic wonders of Yellowstone and Grand Teton national parks.

The state got its name from the Wyoming Valley of northeastern Pennsylvania, where **Native Americans** in the area had formerly lived. Wyoming comes from a Delaware Indian word meaning, "large plains" or "large meadows."

The Snake River running through Grand Teton National park.

Fast Facts

WYOMING

Capital and Largest city
Cheyenne (50,008 people)
Area
96,988 square miles
(251,198 sq km)
Population
493,782 people
Rank: 50th
Statehood
July 10, 1890
(44th state admitted)
Principal rivers
Bighorn River, Green River,
North Platte River
Highest point
Gannett Peak;
13,804 feet (4,207 m)
Motto
Equal rights
Song
"Wyoming"
Famous People
"Buffalo Bill" Cody, Esther
Morris, Nellie Tayloe Ross

*S*tate Flag

*I*ndian Paintbrush

*M*eadowlark

*C*ottonwood

About Wyoming

The Cowboy State and Equality State

Detail area

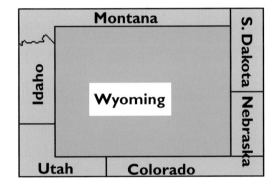

Wyoming's abbreviation

Borders: west (Idaho, Utah), north (Montana), east (South Dakota, Nebraska), south (Utah, Colorado)

Nature's Treasures

The beautiful state of Wyoming has many treasures in its state. In fact, not too many places in the entire world have more treasures than Wyoming.

There are scenic mountains, pretty valleys and canyons, huge dams, thick forests, rich **minerals**, vast farmland, and even deserts in this large state. The treasure filled state is so wonderful that the United States government made Yellowstone the first national park.

Yellowstone National Park has incredible **geysers**, falls, and hot springs. In the Grand Teton National Park there are many peaks that are over 10,000 feet (3,048 m) high.

Many of the towering mountains in the state are forested. Some of the trees are pine, spruce, and fir. Wyoming also has lots of grassland for **grazing** cattle and sheep.

The dams in the state are an awesome site. The most famous is the Buffalo Bill Dam on the Shoshone River near Cody. Gold, oil, gas, and silver have all been found in Wyoming.

Castle geyser, Yellowstone National Park.

Beginnings

The area now called Wyoming was first settled by **Native Americans**. Many people passed through Wyoming on their way to other areas. Most of the historic treks went through Wyoming.

Robert Campbell and William Sublette were the first non-Native American **settlers** to stay in Wyoming in 1834. White settlers began moving to Wyoming. They were mostly fur traders and trappers. Most of these settlers came from eastern states and from Texas.

For many years the Wyoming region was divided into two parts. There was the western area and the eastern area. Finally, in 1868, both sections came together into the Wyoming Territory.

Wyoming was unlike other areas. In 1869, women were allowed to vote, which was unheard of in those days. Then in 1870, women were allowed on juries. These rights were taken away in 1871.

On July 10, 1890, Wyoming became the 44th state in the country. Most people in the early days of the state were fur traders, trappers, or ranchers. Some worked in the oil **industry**, or were gold **miners**.

Fur trappers bringing home a bear.

B.C. to 1834

Early Land and People

During the Ice Age, many thousands of years ago, Wyoming was covered by ice and glaciers. Many years later the ice began to melt and the land of Wyoming began to form.

The first known people to live in and have settlements in Wyoming were **Native Americans**. Some of them were the Crow, Arapaho, Shoshone, and Cheyenne.

1807: John Colter is the first European to **explore** Wyoming.

1834: Robert Campbell and William Sublette build the first long lasting trading post in Wyoming.

Wyoming

B.C. to 1834

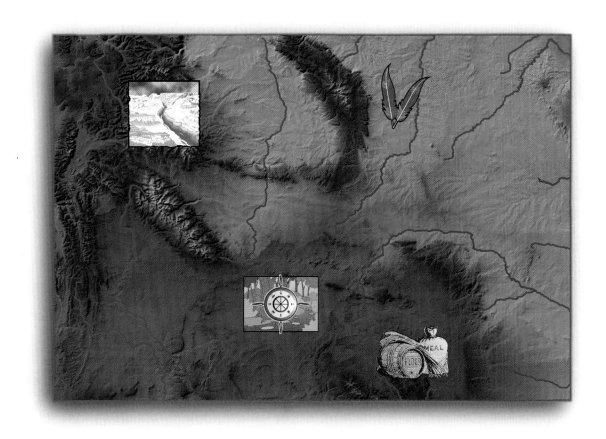

1868 to 1890

Territory to Statehood

 1868: The Territory of Wyoming is created. Cheyenne becomes the capital in 1869.

 1872: Yellowstone National Park opens, making it the first national park in the United States.

 1887: The University of Wyoming opens at Laramie.

 1890: Wyoming becomes the 44th state on July 10.

Wyoming

1868 to 1890

1924 to Present

Present-Day Wyoming

1924: Nellie Tayloe Ross is elected the first woman **governor** in the United States.

1951: Uranium deposits are found in Wyoming.

1966: Canyon National Recreation Area is created. It covers over 63,000 acres in both Wyoming and Montana.

1988: The worst forest fires in Wyoming since the 1950s burn millions of acres, including Yellowstone National Park.

Wyoming

1924 to Present

17

Wyoming's People

There are less than 500,000 people living in the state of Wyoming. It has the least amount of people in the country. The first known people to live in Wyoming were **Native Americans**.

Many well-known people have come from Wyoming. Nellie Tayloe Ross was elected the **governor** of Wyoming in 1924. She was the first woman governor in the United States.

Esther H. Morris moved to Wyoming in 1869 with her husband in search of gold. She pushed for women's rights, especially the right to vote. In 1870, she was chosen to be justice of the peace of South Pass City, Wyoming. She was the first woman ever to do that.

American scout and showman Buffalo Bill Cody spent much of his life in Wyoming. After touring

Wyoming with his famed Wild West tour, like so many, Cody thought the state was beautiful. He founded the town of Cody. Cody built the TE Ranch outside of Cody where he lived and relaxed.

Other famous people from the state include sportscaster Curt Gowdy, **Native American** chief Spotted Tail, and authors Thurman Arnold and Mary Roberts Rinehart.

Buffalo Bill Cody

Nellie Tayloe Ross

Splendid Cities

Most people in Wyoming live in small, **rural** towns. The biggest city in the state has around 50,000 people.

Cheyenne is the largest city and the capital of Wyoming. Cheyenne was the first settlement in Wyoming and almost the name of the state. It was named after the **Native Americans** that lived and hunted in Wyoming.

Cheyenne is located in the southeastern corner near the Colorado **border**. The world's largest rodeo is staged in Cheyenne during Frontier Days, which is a summer festival.

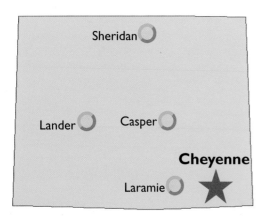

Casper is the second largest city with just under 50,000 people. It lies near the center of the state on the North Platte River. Many people visit the dude ranches here.

20

Laramie is the third largest city, having around 25,000 people. The city is just northwest of Cheyenne. The city attracts people for its mountains, forests, and the University of Wyoming.

A few other cities in Wyoming include Sheridan, Green River, Evanston, and Lander.

A statue in front of the Wyoming State Capitol in Cheyenne.

ESTHER HOBART MORRIS
PROPONENT OF THE LEGISLATIVE ACT WHICH
IN 1869 GAVE DISTINCTION TO THE TERRITORY OF
WYOMING
AS THE 1ST GOVERNMENT IN THE WORLD TO GRANT
WOMEN EQUAL RIGHTS

Wyoming's Land

Wyoming has some of the most beautiful land in the country. There are mountains, forests, lakes, rivers, valleys, and national parks. The state's land is divided into two regions.

The Rocky Mountains region covers the western and central parts of Wyoming. This region has many mountains separated by wide valleys. In the northern part of the land are the large ranges of the Middle Rockies—the Absaroka and Bighorn mountains. Between these mountains is the Bighorn River.

In the northwestern corner of the Rocky Mountains is Yellowstone National

Park. This is a high plateau that extends north and west into Montana and Idaho.

The highest point in the state, Gannett Peak, towers over the area.

The other region in the state is the Great Plains. This area covers the eastern side of Wyoming. The area is mostly rolling stretches of grassland, with few trees, and little rainfall.

This region is known for having the western slopes of the Black Hills, which are mostly in South Dakota. It also has the Belle Fourche River, which is the lowest point in the state.

Beaver Lake, Grand Teton National Park.

Wyoming at Play

The people of Wyoming and the many people who visit the state have a lot of things to do and see. There are usually more visitors in this wonderful state than there are people living there.

For many years, people have enjoyed the historic sites, mountains, rivers, lakes, and national parks. One of the most colorful attractions to the state is dude ranching. Dude ranches are places where **tourists** can enjoy the old wild west ways, ride horses, and stay on a ranch.

Native Americans made Wyoming their hunting ground to survive. Today, thousands of tourists each year visit the state to hunt for sport. Some of the animals hunted are antelope, moose, mountain sheep, elk, bear, and deer.

Of course, the scenic wonders of Yellowstone and Grand Teton national parks are not only the largest **tourist** sites in the state, but also in the entire world. Other popular places to see are Devils Tower National Monument and Fort Laramie National Historic Site.

The towering mountains in the state make for good hiking, biking, and sightseeing. Jackson Hole offers some of the best skiing in the country. People also enjoy fishing and rafting.

There's lots of space in Wyoming to ride horses.

Wyoming at Work

The people of Wyoming must work to make money. Because there are not many large cities, most people from the state work in small **rural** areas.

Many people in Wyoming work in the **mining industry**. Oil, natural gas, coal, clay, iron ore, and uranium are also mined in Wyoming. People also work in manufacturing, and logging.

Many people in Wyoming are farmers and ranchers. The best business for farmers is the sale of cattle, sheep, and wool. Other farmers grow **crops** like sugar beets, corn, beans, and potatoes.

Because **tourism** is a large business in Wyoming, many people from the state work in service. People that work in service work in restaurants, **resorts**, or hotels.

The wonderful state of Wyoming offers many different things to do and see. Because of its natural beauty, people, land, and national parks, Wyoming is a great state to visit, live, work, and play.

An oil drilling rig in Wyoming.

Fun Facts

• The state of Wyoming was almost called Cheyenne. That was the name of one of the **Native American** tribes who lived in the area. Cheyenne was the name given to the first large settlement in the state. Today, Cheyenne is the largest city and the capital of Wyoming.

• Wyoming has many different nicknames. Some are the Cowboy State, the Sagebrush State, and the Big Wyoming State. Its most often used nickname is the Equality State. It got the nickname for supporting equal rights for women. Wyoming was the first state to allow women the right to vote and hold political office.

• The state of Wyoming is known for doing things first. They had the first woman **governor** and justice of the peace in the country. They were the first to allow women to serve on juries. Wyoming also had the first national park and national forest in the United States.

•In the movie, *Close Encounters of the Third Kind*, Devils Tower was the landing spot for aliens from outer space. Devils Tower was the first national monument in 1906.

Devils Tower, Wyoming.

Glossary

Agriculture: another name for farming.

Border: neighboring states, countries, or waters.

Crops: the vegetables or fruit that farmers grow on their farms to sell.

Descendants: people who are related to others who lived a long time ago.

Explorers: people that are some of the first to discover and look over land.

Geyser: a hole in the ground that sends up fountains of hot water and steam.

Governor: the highest elected official in the state.

Graze: animals eating grass.

Industry: many different types of businesses.

Minerals: things found in the earth, such as rock, diamonds, or coal.

Miners: people who work underground to get minerals.

Native Americans: the first people who were born and lived in North America.

Petroleum: also known as oil. An oily liquid that is obtained from wells drilled in the ground. It is used to make gasoline, fuel oils, and other products.

Population: the number of people living in a certain place.

Resort: a place to vacation that has fun things to do.

Rural: outside of the city.

Settlers: people that move to a new land where no one has lived before and build a community.

Tourism: a business that serves people who are traveling for pleasure, and visiting places of interest.

Tourists: people who travel for pleasure.

Internet Sites

Bring Back the Bison-Wyoming
http://www.evanstonwy.com/bb-bison/
Bring Back the Bison is a non-profit environmental organization dedicated to preserving the Yellowstone bison herd and to bring back wild bison herds on our nation's public lands–through education and responsible management.

Big Horn Mountains
http://www.buffalo.com/Bighorns/
Welcome! to Wyoming's Big Horn Mountain Country! We are located in the north-central region of Wyoming. Our location makes the Big Horn Mountain Country region the access route to America's most scenic and pristine mountain regions. This web site was created to provide access to regional information resources in the Big Horn Mountain Country.

These sites are subject to change. Go to your favorite search engine and type in Wyoming for more sites.

PASS IT ON

Tell Others Something Special About Your State

To educate readers around the country, pass on interesting tips, places to see, history, and little unknown facts about the state you live in. We want to hear from you!

To get posted on ABDO & Daughters website, E-mail us at "mystate@abdopub.com"

Index